The Brighter House

The Brighter House

Kim Garcia

WHITE PINE PRESS / BUFFALO, NEW YORK

White Pine Press
P.O. Box 236
Buffalo, New York 14201

www.whitepine.org

Publication of this book was made possible, in part, with public funds from the New York State Council on the Arts, a State Agency.

Acknowledgments:
My thanks to the editors and publishers of the following journals and chapbooks where these poems first appeared, some in slightly different form: *Atlanta Review*: "Transfusion, 2 pm." *Bellingham Review*: "Paschal Triptych." *Birmingham Poetry Review*: "Unicorn and Virgin, Cloisters Tapestries," "Black Madonna." *Cimarron Review*: "Tales of the Sisters" (appeared in a different form). *Comstock Review*: "Grief," "It's simpler." *Crazyhorse*: "the mystic crucifixion by Tintoretto." *Dogwood*: "Annunciation." *Free Verse*: "Lilies of the Field." *Hunger Mountain*: "Prayer on the Feast of the Assumption," "Rumpelstiltskin." *Inkwell*: "Miracle." *Iodine Poetry Journal*: "Strangers." *The Ledge*: "1943, How We Got Made." *Nimrod*: "How I Learned to Talk," "Ophelia Emerges from the River, Unscathed."
Acknowledgments continue on page 80.

Cover image : "Tree Sacrifice" by Joan Braun. Used by permission of the artist.

ISBN 978-1-935210-89-4

Library of Congress Control Number: 2015959243

Most importantly, my thanks to the many friends, family, teachers and colleagues (often one category) who have contributed generously to this work and the larger life of poetry in which it has been nourished—you know who you are! In particular, I wish to express my deep gratitude to those who handled this manuscript in its awkward adolescence—Emilie Boon, Liza Rutherford, Allison Adair, Sue Roberts, Skye Shirley, Brook Emery, Holly Iglesias, John Anderson, Jim Henle, Gary Whited, Rachel Kadish, and the poets and editors of the 2013 Colrain Manuscript Intensive—for insightful readings and edits that nurtured it towards completion.

I'm very grateful to Jericho Brown for choosing this manuscript, to Dennis Maloney and Elaine LaMattina at White Pine Press for their careful work, to Larry Richman for his sensitive proofreading, and to Keun Young Bae and Sarah Cassatly for keeping the process humane and organized.

My thanks to the Hambidge Center for the Arts for numerous essential residencies throughout the gestation of this book.

And finally I want to thank Sarah, Michael and Frank for teaching me everything I know about love, forgiveness and belonging.

For my families

I inherited a dark wood where I seldom go. But a day will come when the dead and the living change places. Then the wood will start moving. We are not without hope. The most serious crimes will remain unsolved in spite of the efforts of many policemen. In the same way there is somewhere in our lives a great unsolved love. I inherited a wood, but today I'm walking in the other wood, the light one. All the living creatures that sing, wiggle, wag and crawl! It's spring and the air is very strong. I have graduated from the university of oblivion and am as empty-handed as the shirt on the washing-line.

Tomas Tranströmer, "Madrigal"

Contents

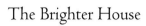

The Brighter House

Tales of the Sisters: Snow

I am five. I am watching strange, silent movements through a window of paper snowflakes that I have made and glued to the panes. Sharp cuts made once, fanning out in patterns that duplicate and duplicate.

My dark sister is beaten in that first, beautiful, wished-for snow. My father beats her with snow chains on her shoulders, her back, through her dark green winter coat. He beats one sister and quiets three.

He's careful. She does not bleed or bruise. I knew my sister's body. I would have seen, but there was nothing to see. My father did not leave marks. Just a scuffled place in the snow,

one red glove where the black asphalt showed through, snow melted away with the heat of her body. A memory of my sister's face not frightened as it might have been, but hard and concentrated as it often was, acolyte somber.

The clumsy back swing of my father's arm, working with the momentum of the iron chains, in that silent world outside the window. Fragments, as quiet as church.

The chains will not make a sound, not on the snow—the beautiful, called-for snow, or on her body, or on the asphalt that shows where her wriggling legs have scuffled against the ground, turning away and away,

shielding one part of her body and then another.

*

When I was a child I believed one day my sister would walk into the ring, like the matadors she loved, in a jacket of embroidery and mirror, in the pink stockings and slippers of a ballerina.

I believed her pure, sharp hate would go in like a blade; the bull would breathe his own blood and fall, silent in the thick drift of sawdust; and the men on horses would tie the back legs to a harness and

simply drag the dead thing away.

In My City of Z, Forgiveness

In the City of Z, I was scarred—three lines, sternum to solar plexus.
They wept and festered and would not heal. *How else can you be beautiful?*
asked the angels of that place. I had hoped for something more

than my own body handed back to me, still barren, still bargaining.
My mouth was stuffed with manioc. My belly gave up its worms,
still I would not abandon the pictures hope twisted from my dreams.

They threatened to crush my skull, to feed me to the fish. I pressed
small children for a word of the world in the other country, a physics
of speech not equal but opposite. So they teased me with nonsense,

birdsong, their own alliterative names made strange by my longing
to speak strange, be strange, all at once familiar, while my abdomen
bloomed—egg-laying insects, boring to blood, unhinging the last bone.

I kept a final word under my tongue, belligerent child. Shook my head.
I didn't want to. Wouldn't. Not even silence could enter my lips, gentle
as she was. I had paid my way cross-river. I had to be worth something.

How I Learned to Talk

The road had been oiled to keep
the dust down when the truck came that August,
and the man opened his door and asked
directions. I balanced a bowl of raspberries

against my hip, still straight, torso a thin tube
with a hole down the center, like a whistle.
He was kinder than I'd imagined he'd be.
Get in here, he said. *Show me the way.*

I thought strangers would look hard and eager
like my father, like my mother
when she caught you doing what she knew
you'd do, you were always doing or wanted

to do. He was more like me, dry mouth
tasting the tang of his idling engine, the blue
bowl impossibly bright with berries.
As though I could wake up now—suddenly.

A mouth
closed over my whisper. The flesh grew
around the hard white core of want.
And where I pulled the fruit away—

turned on my heel and ran, scattering
berries my mother would send me back for,
to pick out of the oily dust and rinse—

a hollow where I put my tongue.

And in the beginning was all the after

i.

I couldn't understand what He said   just infernal clacking
coming   out from darkness, going   into darkness

      And then you were there, feathered and formed.
And I was there—webbed, as usual. And I was teaching
you the way of something hairless, but you weren't listening.
You knew everything
          you had would grow back. The sky
was still there, the air, the feathers and the wax,
which was me melting. Which was us melting
which was a problem for you, somewhat,
         until with a plop, and the encircling rings
of my disappearance, I vanished into the still pond
making too much noise, too much ripple
despite all my efforts to maintain the void.

ii.

On the second day we were at the gate. The angel
was saying what people in uniforms always say:

It wasn't his rule, he was only enforcing it.
I could see you were about to offer him something

under the table, a bribe maybe. No money had changed
hands, but it was in your minds. He hesitated,

you turned your hands, palms up, two pink dogs
begging, and then I knew everything

that would come after—after he nodded
and passed you the torch, to remind me

we would go forward carrying Paradise,
falling over ourselves, and never get the Fucking

Thing off our skins, no matter
how we rolled.

iii.
In the third act, God was played by my father.
He was dead, and he wasn't coming back.
He lay three days in the freezer. His skin

was packed with ice crystals, like a partially
thawed steak. His top denture was loose.
He was faintly yellow, like an old book.

His words were in my mouth, his teeth in my mouth,
I tasted his bitterness, his salt. I retched, and it sounded
like this: Lucky, Lucky, Lucky.

iv.
Four horses, one chariot.
Four wings over the covenant
where the angels bow down.
Four senses in one sight: salt, sunlight
whistling at the window, and
in a single hot shaft, the scent of light.
Who can say what is a blessing?

18

I'm gifted with curses.
Four guardians at the four gates
holding back Paradise, damming its flood.

v.

The fifth of bourbon, five chestnuts
each with its false burl, five digits, counting,
the palmer's kiss, five acts, five orifices,
five rings on the fifth day, to collar each finger, fifth child,
fifth wheel, fifth hope, last swallow, bottom of the fifth.

vi.

And then the dead were raised, the winds
blew from six directions, and every seal
was opened. Words returned to the mouths
of their owners. Names were named.
There were no surprises. But it went on
and on, six days and nights.
                    Sixty times six.
And every name read was not mine,
and every face was not mine. And I said,
"I get it. Okay. Not me. Not mine,"
and the angel said, "Sit down.
You're not done reading."

vii.

We'd like to rest, like to turn back,
the way you turn back a sheet, smooth it—
the pillow a cheek, the quilt a hand, the dust

of the day, turned back, back, on itself, the dust ruffle
hanging, hanging limp, the dust stilled
along the baseboards, under the corners more dust
sitting soberly in our chairs. Everything is saying

goodnight. Everything is coming to rest. Descending
the way cold does, layer by layer, a thermal inversion
where heat rises off a torch, breaking the ribs, stirring
the organs, already cold, with a toe.
                                            You're back,
better than ever, seventh son of the seventh son.
You're lucky like that.

Oil

I slipped in unwanted, like silverfish,
fleas, a blocked pore, any small
annoyance that beggars
explanation. I wanted to be

algae. The velvety soup
an endless mouth over the clear
breast of water. Green pond's eye.
It neither toils nor spins.

I lived in Texas, catching rides
that took longer than I thought.
And death never caught me,
easy as I was to catch.

The nine ready virgins
have gone in with their bridegroom,
lamps lit, each one a life
I might have lived.

I am loose at the joints.
Walked every bare socket,
swung every dry bone.

Strangers

The man with the grass truck, for instance,
looking in on me through the car window.
I sat in my robe passenger side, engine humming
while my mother went for my prescription.

I was pale, very still. I was always
sick in those days. His eye moved
over my shoulders, into the folds of my robe,
a ticklish insect-footed sensation on my skin.

I stared back. Probably I flirted.
I don't remember, but I did things like that,
swallowed whatever came in the capsules.
I was pale, and my eyes were almost black.

My mother came out of the drugstore.
Who called who? He came down
from the load of sod he was pitchforking
to two black men below. They spoke.

Our lawn was dead.
The car was dying.
She wanted grass.
I was useless to her.

A few days later he came with a load.
After he laid the sod, he drank
a glass of lemonade at the kitchen table
with my mother. Then he took me to the drive-in.

We saw a trucker picture. *Convoy*, I think,
and he didn't handle me much
or force his mouth over my mouth
or speak in any way about the sod he'd unloaded
all day in Texas heat—for what?

To buy me popcorn,
to run his arm along the back
of the vinyl single seat of his pick-up
and stare in silence at a girl
stiff and scared in the seat beside him,
not knowing what she was beginning or ending.

When the movie ended
he took me home
and walked me to the door
like a real date would have done.

And the only thing he got for what he'd paid
my mother was one brief run of his warm palm
from my hip to my bra strap
along my thick, fifteen year old waist.

Which couldn't have been much a thrill
for a full grown man.

My mother was in bed. No.
She was up. Watching television,
sitting in the chair she'd rocked me in
as a child. Outside the sprinkler's steady tick
broke suddenly into a run and return.
The peepers spoke under the damp leaves,

to a steady tap of beetles against the yellow light.
Moths folded flat against the dark siding.

There'd be new grass in my mother's voice
as she looked up from her lap
where she'd have some work,
some bill to worry or dress to mend,
and ask, "What did you do?"

Just beyond the window lay the lawn, her lawn,
which would be lovely today, tomorrow
and years from now. Children changed.
You fed them and put a roof over their heads,
and one night your daughter might walk in
and look at you like a stranger.

Miracle

So awkwardly arranged that she must walk with one hand extended
       like the blind, anticipating touch in a world full of surface
balancing a bucket of lake water half as heavy as she is, a strange S curve
       in the spine, torqued.

       The air smells like moss over granite flecked with mica, a living
green skin to the solid stone. Just as the pure water where it lips the shore
       thickens, rises eagerly. Matter aspiring.
She's carrying a fish head in that bucket. She wants it to grow back a tail,
       swim again. She's praying for it.

The compass will turn in her hand. The stars circle the humble dippers, rivers flow
       from broken foam, smoothed over rocks at the headwaters, gather
into unbroken pools, pulse back into the springs. In the dark the tree bark will flicker
       and suddenly return the light it received all day. And everything
we were ever grateful for will happen again and again and again.

In the night a raccoon—with intelligent hands, so articulate they might
       be the mind itself, turning the partial in jointed palms—
lifts the fish head in its mouth and returns to its kits, each a hot ball of fur
       and intention. They rush and retreat at a strange smell so different
from the milk of their mother. Then fall on the open eye and consume it.

       When the girl comes to get the bucket in the morning, won't she
think that a miracle has taken place? The fish has grown its tail, turned
       the bucket with thrashing, flopping its way to the lake?
She crouches by the bucket and considers it. The cabin's screen
       door slams. Her mother hangs wet towels on the line.

       In a minute her mother will say *go make your bed, put up the cereal.*
The miracle will be over. It's already over. She looks at the empty bucket
       wishing the fish were dead, wishing she were praying again.

Tales of the Sisters: Bees

"Be still," my light sister teaches. She whispers. She teaches me to blend into the white walls, to make myself dull, to slow my breathing when I am afraid, to lie still as snow.

She sits on my bed by the nightlight and shows me a pamphlet Baptists have given her. One page shows her heart before God—a minus sign sitting on a chair. Pluses and minuses whirl around it like confused bees.

And on the next, her heart after God. There is a cross on the chair now, there are no minuses, and pluses are crowded up on the white page like good children, waiting in a circle for a story.

"That's the throne of my heart," she whispers, so only God and I can hear, "That's a place no one can see."

Rumpelstiltskin

After the loud and painful popping, the mess,
the whole stink of his rage, the mopping up,
walls washed down, curtains rehung
the rug—obviously—was done for and this
too, whole rooms of straw, damp and molding
not even the look of gold.
                    I had to sell
off the jewelry, things I'd had in the family
for years, a piece of land I had never seen
just heard of, my horse. I mucked out
the house, but still the smell of barn, of rooms
unused and unwanted, and the king, paupered
dowerless, stood teaching our son to say,
"I thought you were magic."
                    I could go back
out the way I'd come—the servants' entrance
where my father first peddled his lies. He knew
what I was, what I'd be willing to do.
What mother promises her own child to a stranger?
My God, when they put me out the sluice and into
the street, what a story I'll have to tell, with bells,
with tears in all the right places.

The Little Golden Books

I.
The Toad Princess

The mother lid was screwed down tight
over all the world's fireflies, their bright tails—
but the blue dusk escaped her, wrapped me up
in a cool skin, pulsing as a toad's throat, smell

of rotten leaves, where the toads hid. Hunting
in my nightgown, bare-legged on summer nights
in Texas, piercing bug-shrill, only the water
inside our skins, quiet to match the quiet

of the waiting toads. Heat brought their crooked
legs, their self-clawed four-fingered hands, to rustle
the old leaves hustled off the branches by the new
into piles in the corners of the yard no father mowed.

Compost pile turrets, the white of cold rot, snap
of cockroach backs under out feet or June bugs
against the porch lights. Flashlights caught the gold
of the eyes. Quick hands wet with the clean smell

of their pee—like water over warm stone, the wriggling
of their bodies as we held them up in the air by the base
of their jaws and loved them—more wonderful because
they could not love us, and more wonderfully still

could not hurt us by that.

2.
Queen Babel

I made this too-muchness of me. She wouldn't pay for it,
she said, couldn't keep replacing shoes, buying new, just
because I went and outgrew them.

Let me love you, O endless
      expanding bone. O projects
            O masticated mouthful of meat, unswallowable.

Eat it, she said, as I telescoped and twisted in my chair, skyscrapering
up, a confusion of voices. Eat it. Her hand at the hinge
of my jaw. Tomorrow we could be on the streets.

3.
Little Man

On the first day we stood in lines
      rubbing a dime and a quarter together
            breathing sour milk, steamed bread, tomato paste.

A woman in a hairnet took my money.
      I sucked the ketchup out of the bag.
            My teacher crossed her legs at the head of the table.

On the second day, the boy threw up
      And the teacher said *okay, okay.*
            I darkened the red lines on my paper and forgot my four-times.

On the third day I found an eraser
        shaped like a bandit, smelling like salt and lead.
                I made him a home in my metal desk, the watercolor dish

we never used for his pool, the box of crayons his bed,
        and I loved him very much. Just like that.
                Because I decided to. His broken hand,

head flattened with erasing on one side, hole up his rubber butt
        the ugly leer of a paid fool on his face. I love you,
                I love you, little man, please never die.

For my father and the cancer that killed him

                                        Once
in a drainage ditch I saw a duck and hawk
rolling, like wrestlers—old Greeks—to the death,
and the duck was taking his dying hard. It took

a long, silent time for the sugar to run out

in its muscles, for the hawk to find the place
between its neck and back, to pierce the artery,
open the blood gate, let out the fight and begin
                                        to feed.

1943, How We Got Made

My father led her down
into the basement of the Chicago warehouse
took off his shirt.

And my mother
tucked up her legs under her skirt
pretending to be scared

as he bludgeoned rats, big as small dogs,
and threw their bodies into the furnace.
The stench of burnt fur, blood, coal

chummed the air. What was
hungry in them rose and fed.
Every violence, even then, was conceived.

Then he put his shirt back on.
She checked her stockings, her teeth,
while he got paid in a pile of ones.

Outside, service stars were going up
in windows all over Chicago.
Boys coming home a hand short.

Where would they go now?
They had money, gas for the car,
and clean, white sugar.

Tales of the Sisters: The Walrus

He walks us along the sparkling sea. Sparkling like champagne, he says.
His thick moustache brushes the top of our wrists. His teeth are heavy. They are

gold. His words are like saltwater, thicker, more buoyant than the water our
mother gives us to drink. We walk along the edge of the sea while the tide is

out, and the empty shells and clear bodies of the jellyfish—white digestive
systems floating in a thick cloud of mucus—are reminders of something

which I have made to slip my mind, but will return, perhaps, with the tide.
"I'm hungry," he says. He holds us by the hand, hard.

"We are so intimate," he says spinning his private verse, "We could be more
so." We must complete the couplet. We must return that tide.

He eats us whole. Gray oyster flesh, smelling of the sea. He sucks the juice,
called nectar, from our shells. Takes the round, white pearl of our kingdom

within. Rolls it over his thick, pink tongue. Crushes it to powder between
his back molars. He opens his mouth.

"See?" he says, smiling, "Just dust."

Thor

He had everything to hand, and what reach!
His anger burned out and back to him, still hot
to be caught in an iron mitt that made a clumsy
hoof of every gesture. How he pawed me.

The hammer was dwarfish work, the dark-smelted
gold of a greed so solitary and slavering
that its violence was a cleansing,
fashioned to fly across the vast inner hall

and strike the sinew vibrating there
waiting to be plucked, strung tight
from thought to belly. He knew where the dragon
lay, gnawing at the tree that lifted the gods. Don't

ask me to speak. His weight lies on my tongue, constant
correction. *Dumb.* A felted hammer on razored strings.

You're All the Gods to Me

We are one whole sight, one blindness
together, yours on the right, mine the left,
each paid an eye, telling the pictures.
I hung three days letting the past—a scent,
memory of a scent—touch, until I saw
sound, heard sight. Bare branches settled me
with their language, wind drifting the dark
as I hung from your tree and read the All-Father.

Current ran up from the ground to meet you,
in sandy soil, your reach left fingers of glass.
Late at night the restless thunder of ice
in your old-fashioned as you sat on my bed
breathing, breathing, until I lost my breath
counting the seconds until the light fell.

Transfusion, 2 p.m.

My father is white paper
despite the day's transfusion.
Red bag fat as a tick
mouth-deep in his pale arm,
We have not escaped the need
to heal by blood.

Father's Day cards, get well,
thinking of you. I can't find
in myself a single hard word
against the sturdy weave of sentiment
or any human grasping—
the way my father struggles
after the phone, fixed to the rails
of the hospice bed, hand vibrato
as a heart string.

He tells me again about the bike,
repossessed when he was twelve
parents pocketing his pay.
That hungry boy is still
yelling for candy, for cake
made with butter, goddammit.

Heartless and fey at nineteen
he piloted bombers over Cologne,
flak blooming, black ink in water,
taking off and landing in England's fog.
Night missions, dead buddies,
a gunner who flew drunk.

Once, stationed far north
and fooled by the endless light
he'd tried for breakfast at two a.m.
Locked outside the mess hall, screaming,
You sons of bitches, I'm hungry!
Until the cook came out and said,
You crazy bastard. Don't you know
what time it is?

He needs to rest now, the nurses say,
but what is rest to a man who could not hold
a child on his lap without teasing it,
who into a family of cold anti-Semites
introduced my dark mother as a Jew,
who beat his children so passionately
we had no choice but to love
and fight him doggedly forever?

I hold his hand, adjust the bed,
watch his eyes track the television
broadcasting its strange seeds of desire
on barren ground. He wants one more
of what he knows—one more too—long look
at my daughter, one more visit,
one more kiss. Butter, breakfast, bike.
You crazy bastard, don't you know
what time it is?

This Remains

Death is a child, slipping her hand
in mine, never quite knowing where
we're going, putting everything in her mouth.

I tell her the names of things before
they vanish. She won't remember today
tomorrow. She's never touched the forbidden

tree, never gripped its branch—hard,
screaming *no* when it was too late for no,
too late to save the limb, the leaf, the seed.

Too late for everything but her damp hand,
small and insistent, plucking at my cuff,
taking me to that griefless place she knows

saying *me, me now.*

The Dead in Summer

Awakened again by the hunger shriek—
baby sparrows as their mother returns
with grubs. It's their third summer
to build under our air conditioner.
These are the grandchildren
of that first mistake, not much
to look at—featherless sinew, toothpick
bones, then an ugly molt.

The cold Boston soil is warmed
as it has always been, by breezes
from the Atlantic, coming up the old Trades—
Trinidad, Jamaica, sugar plantations,
terrible histories. Things get better
and then worse again. We can't decide
if the world is warming or cooling.

Even this room is losing its history—
out with the orange chair, $5 at a yard sale,
the kimono my sister suggested I wear
over a thong, a sturdy Swedish horse
(also torii gate orange)—all fading.
Pale photographs of my grandfather
as a clown, arms around unidentified women.

His paint box on a shelf—black face,
white face, a red cylinder of grease paint
for cheek and nose. A safety pin,
a budget book for 1916, hauling
wet laundry with a horse and cart.
He made a bit of money outside Detroit
walking on his hands for the rich.

These are old cities with corrupt unions
and long memories and big suburban Tudors a long walk out
from the factories where the money was made,
where the workers might pick up a brick
or a bar of steel and come after you,
where blacks crossed picket lines
the Irish had made and crossed before them,
where the wealthy measured out their worth
through a system of mating too complicated for God.

What ills was this flesh not heir to?
Furnace burns, boils, a scar from the press
my grandfather worked, tool and die
in Ford's first factories. The heavy thumb
of the rag man who measured out his pennies
and had to be tricked with a bundled brick.
A mad first wife, a young and silent second,
the day his hands gave out long before his hating.

The day is heating up. Mornings like this
it can seem we have escaped the curse, arranged
our pleasures in long, undulating beds.
The birds come back, the sparrows nest,
raise another generation of chicks
deafened by the machinery of staying cool,
while the Norway maples we planned
to pull out of the yard shade the exhausted
daylilies, kill the bloom. Here and there
a burst of orange flames out
in a green dusk that lingers all day.

echo, echo

he fills my eye   beautiful boy in the pool   wash of cataract

cloud circling   crystal palace   pleasure dome   chasm

snow globe of delicate petals   returning to their source

with the scent of ice and fire   then vanilla   pin feathers

dropped vowel by vowel   uncut by consonant   simply

shuttlecock   simply snow   simply cloud   pool   boy   again boy

Sonnet

The cold whip of rail is ice at the last stop, a bit
of steel mesh over the bare bulb of winter, a station

without a master. I need a ticket and tap a man,
parka repaired with duct tape; he turns

an eaten face—one eye over a hole in the sink
of his skull, an almost toothless mouth. Cancer

maybe, that dark harbor, or some other far away,
another-day disaster come suddenly close, possible,

very nearly mine. The blowhole steams. He waits.

I repeat my question, keeping my two eyes

on his one. He tells me to pay on the train, which I do,
while he sits in the next car, eye doubled in the dark glass,

the train passing town, where a single stone marks all the men shifting
toward me in their wet graves—never warmer, never less strange.

We Say

the suffering is over now   isn't it wonderful   we have entered
a new   non-suffering state   already waiting   wet lines hung
for the future happiness   we are now enduring   with its absence

the inevitable act two   where things get
interesting   not now   no we say   not now while
we are happy   but later on

the card is resting on the silver tray   something we read
once   something out of a novel   not quite real   we can forget
the card   the crooked, crabbed script

a visitor   we can turn away   we say   we were out
away   we say   we were happy
we missed you

Tales of the Sisters: Cherries

My dark sister is sixteen, surrounded by trays and tubs of make-up. Green eye shadow, dark eyeliner, blush, a lipstick called Ripe Cherries. Red on her milk glass,

on napkins, red on her teeth, red on her pillow when she comes home late and goes to bed unwashed.

We share a room now that my father has left, now that we live in a house with fewer rooms. My light sister comes home from college now and then, papery and

insubstantial, flickering. Sleeps on a fold-out couch, never unpacks. Smiling, whistling, constantly moving, a stutter of domestic accidents.

My dark sister licks her lips in the bathroom mirror. I sit in my first bra, two slings of cotton fluff, seeing how everything is done. Whatever I do next I'll stiffen into.

It's called popping your cherry, Stupid, not picking it, my dark sister says, *And it's not that complicated.*
My stomach is a gnarled pit. I listen, nod my head, feign

disinterest. Every word she says makes me harder, denser. Sure. I knew boys were like that. I knew that was the deal.

✷

I wake up to red cherry lights swirling the white plaster ceiling and my mother calling my sister by her full name, the way she does when we're really in trouble.

One arms slops over the side of the stretcher, a movie arm, the way you know the bad guy is really dead. They take her away.

My sister comes back to us pumped, vacuumed out, empty as a straw. She puts on her old clothes, old school, old place at the table. Hand-me-downs.

We don't talk about what's happened. I don't say *Why'd you do it where I'd be sure to see?* She doesn't say, *Because I wanted you to remember it.*

I track her with my eyes. Urgent. I want to say, *Don't do that anymore. Don't do anything anymore. Be still.*

Aubade

The trees are heavy with leaf and seed,
waiting for some quick cold unraveling.
I am worn. Up since three
waiting for sleep, and then
no longer waiting. Waiting for life to turn
over a new leaf, and then not waiting.

There is a soft fold in my belly.
Let me tell the world the way I did
when I had small children. If I were dying
tomorrow I would be bitter. I would
buy a brighter house. I would leave bad
memories. I would be the brighter house.

I lie awake, thinking about that golden boy.
Such a walk he had! Careless about his bones,
the strain on the ligaments—like he never heard
about sun damage, scars, inherited curses,
bone fractures that don't heal.
Sometimes I just lie on the couch.
I take back time, and nothing hurts me.

Blessing

for my sisters

A lost cup, broken bowl, and the fundamentals—DNA,
Imagination, my beloveds quick and dead;

little ones, a fist curled in my palm, quick
silverfish of possibility, rotting weave,

the woof, black dog
and far mountain, concealed in clouds;

a field of white plastic bags, garbage
and failure and reeking regret,

acceptance, hot and fallow
compost of all kinds, green, white-hot

blisters in hell's hotel, vibrato,
more vibrato, coloratura stripped

of the colora, the nose, a twitching
limb, the phantom,

all things reached, reaching, the longing
to reach, failure to reach,

yielding, a far door slamming
open and shut until it's torn from its jamb

raspberry, cascade berry, logan, boysen, plum
the tastes of *rosa creativa*, the compass

magenta and magellanic, champagne
in the womb, your first kiss maternal;

after a tourniquet of despair, slaughter of newborns,
the return of the cold

spring's blinding lip, sun over snow,
a pour of hope smelted

into something stranger: new worlds.
All this I wish you, pilgrims.

Unicorn and Virgin, Cloisters Tapestries

for my husband

I was, as you said, very strange.
Pale and larval, like something flayed.
Lips blue, head heavy with hard want.
You loved when I shivered under your palm.

When you took me home to meet your mother
she turned my head, side to side, in her hands.
"Very white," she said, "What is it?"
My hooves turned to glue.

Sweet sterile spring. It could not last.
There was only one of my kind
weak-kneed and willing, easy
to catch and band, to yoke.

You marked my flank with a single lily.
I was written in your book.

Fixed

A jittery blue horizon line purpled by a mountain's soft shoulder, smudged as a bruise. Then the sun came over the ridge, and everything lit up—green needle-pricks of new leaf, tracks of dogwood, more urgent than addiction, but shooting up with the same sweet rush, a wanting prayer-humbled, its own answer, germ of next need already packed in the moment's ovum, twitching.

A nest of baby birds washed out, but the parents go on singing after storm, swoop down, powdery moths in their beaks, spooning them fresh into open vein-blue throats, weak after a night of shrieking, of being colder than ever, trembling as lightning revealed them—flash by flash—helpless in the runoff, heavy heads, wing-fins paddling air, clawing mud. That's over now, the father

is forcing the still-living moths into their throats, beating hope into them as he crushes the flutter. It's good, this junk, this bread. Belly full of delicate leg, needle-fine antennae. They call louder, want it harder, deeper, always more.

Annunciation

for my daughter

They say Brother Lawrence
was converted when he looked
at a single leafless branch
and saw blossom under bark.

I see fruit in bud,
burst skin,
circling wasps
the congealing sweetness

When I wrap a flashlight
in swaddling and lay it
in a manger of cardboard brick

I see you. I am suffused
with tenderness. I see
all the small bones

each as sharp as a needle,
a whisker of glass—this play
is spine and thorn, hinged

as those toys that expand
like a lung into spheres
and then contract to hard stars.

Prayer on the Feast of the Assumption

A dead mother stirs, sits up, rubs her knees, puts on
the heavy wig, the burka, the whole body bag

that contains her radiance. Steps down and rests
her hands on my shoulders. I ask not to be given

away, to stay under her palms, to be over. But she
is already unzipping the river, already rising. *Swim.*

Tales of the Sisters: Atlantis

The weight of the water at the bottom of the sea crushes the air out of our bones. It is a desert, an endless overabundance of just one thing.

We speak a dead language grown cryptic with disuse, peer into windows on dead streets, tell stories about what might have happened there, all of it distorted with current.

The weight of the water presses our jaws forward, out of our mouths, until they're nothing but teeth. Eyes protrude. A cord of nerves extrudes from the brain and produces a ball of light. We feed by this.

We know we are monsters.

We move very little, hypnotized by our own bubbles—stowaways from the world of oxygen—that rise slow and guilty to the surface miles away.

There is no sound but the sound of the bubbles leaving our mouths. The sound is something like a soft purr. Something like a faint tearing.

He does not need to say to us, "This is your home. This is where you belong." We know no other paradise. We are just one flesh—my father's awesome, ungraspable body.

The Child Steps into the Dream Water
to Declare Her Existence

I advance slowly over the pontoons, backs of alligators,
bridge of turtles. It is night. Far off some people are singing

around a fire. They are passing the bottle. But the child
is sober, ruffed in starched linen, pale and Spanish as a Velásquez

asked to lift the corpse of Count Ortiz, not hoping on the heaven
that swirls around the rising soul's skirts, bound to the sinuous frame,

where I tread water, a bath of black lacquer. Beautiful river,
terrible river, until the hand I am half expecting takes me by the heel

and pulls me under.
            I will go back to this country where a face is a song,
a song is a child, where the child is my water, where I am broken.

Ophelia Emerges From the River, Unscathed

Two boys, two minds, followed me home through streams so clear
I could see just how wet I'd get. The last bit cost me. I writhed on
a sandbank while they watched, growing older, darker, more beautiful.

They followed me to the house, my childhood kitchen with slats
of beach light where walls had been. They harried a ball of white light
from room to room and out, where it hovered, twinkling,
until I shut it in the door.

Caught in the jamb it was skull and bones, manic as a set of wind-up
teeth. I took hold of the skull, turned its face to me, saying in a
mother's voice, "*You don't want to be old. You want to be young*"

and threw it into a square of raked earth dark as coffee grounds
and buried it. When I returned home, the boys had become men.
They had capes, boots, beards. They were tall and serious. Silk
merchants, travelers.

There were still new worlds. One would find them;
one would stay with me.

Black Madonna

for Sarah

I.
I was born in the Lenten dark
in a cloud of gas, unauthorized,

a blue and bloodless Wednesday
like the butchered and flayed

lamb I once saw in Greece.
Blood lacquer pooling at the neck,

Venetian red under black,
on the steel counter, balanced

by a vase of Easter roses.

I cried and they put me
to my mother's drugged breast

to suck first cream, the color
of yolk. My mother was silent.

Nothing leapt up.
She said she never felt so old.

I rested in the folds framed
by my brothers and sisters,

begotten and begotten and begotten
the old forced march.

2.

When my much-desired
        daughter crushed the bones
of her skull through my body gate,
        I knew I could never hold her.

The midwife crouched on the floor
        between my feet. Shrugged
as I screamed,
        I can't, I can't.

Her face dark and tender,
        like the Black Madonna's.
She knew everything,
        but what could she do?

As the head burnt through
        my bones, coal on tongue,
tearing muscle, making
        each lip speak water and blood,

it turned; and the body
        still resting below my breath
turned with it. And I felt
        the limbs take leave,

touching as they went every bruise,
        every weeping wall
the violence of birth
        had opened.

3.
My womb closed after you,
Lamb, Lacquer, Lenten rose.
The hull you left was like a limb
broken to be straightened again.

What blew through me?
I was opened at every door,
pierced like the Madonna's icon
hidden under a bed during the purges.

Soldiers knifed the feather mattress
and opened mouths, wombs, eyes
in her dark face. Tenderness wells up
in those wounds. They heal and bleed.

Tales of the Sisters: Judgment

End times. Cancer spreads from prostate to bone. It could look like a judgment on him.

From a table by the diner window I see him walk in, moving slowly, painfully, like a diver through water, bloated, papery, head stretched out like a tortoise's.

I'm poleaxed with pity—*Look what you've done. How could you do that to him?* I'm sick on tenderness. All I want to do is forgive.

He holds my hands in his, doesn't let go. Old sales technique. Eyes lock mine. His hands squeeze. We sit. His waffles come. He doesn't let go.

His talk keeps turning to what I write, what my sisters say I write. We are agreed about one thing—I make things up, fictionalize. That's my line and I stick to it. All I want to do is forgive.

I want to talk about his health, about his dying, the only reason I can remember for being here. His hands go on squeezing.

Those terrible things my sisters have said about him. Very unfair, a misunderstanding, worked out, in the past, a pack of damn lies. I keep mopping up with a little rag of forgiveness borrowed from therapy-speak.

"That must have been very hard for you, Dad," I say, sick with pity going cold and my own hypocrisy. Under the table my legs start to shake.

Then he looks better than he has all morning, relaxes, lets go of my hands, sits back, gaze wandering up my shoulder, to the ceiling, like a man having an insight. He leans in, a salesman making concessions, prepared to be fair.

"Now maybe French kissing your sister was bad judgment."

Grief

for my sisters

in that place we squeezed between the trunks, the trees were that close,

an old fog like lichen and moss grew down from the trees, snaked

up the hill, as though there were no summit, never would be a sun,

not the little ball of midday or the heavy yolk of sunrises and sets,

just the bodiless body of not quite seeing, with less room to pass, less

to remember; branches of dead needle and leaf where no sun came,

smell of balsam, fog, and crusts of moss we broke through into streambeds

and rotting log. Then between the trees the ocean—gray as a fogbank,

seagull resting on the wind, a far off shussing, our breathing.

Early Morning

As though my lover placed his cold, chapped hand
against the soft tissue under my ribs, stopping my breath.

As though that silence were an incision
I could step through. Foot-lifted, hand in the flame.

Or as though we were sparrows hopping on the garage roof,
the trees dripping, piercing the gray with silver needles.

A pink magnolia holding up palm after palm of blessing.

Paschal Triptych

I.
Spring's dead child heaves her stone

and the ice of her birthing settles into new joint,
compounding the cold grief of old grievance
making even complaint unbearable. What good luck

to be worn out and beyond worry, frost-plucked
and composted in muck. A thousand stables flow
and the fly-specked dove, dull as a page, circles

the destruction as though it were not destruction,
just the look of spring, the way it will be from now on.

2.
Stranger, this happiness,

a pattern of screen
        knocked loose
letting in the bees
        the busy touch
hum below thought
        unpurposed
flight sounds—small paddles
        making the air batter.
All summer the tick
        of sprinklers
a whine of repair.
        Soon the waxy

brindled cups
        the early fall light,
summer's amber marrow
        still blood warm.

3.
The net is cast

out with its delicate tufts, a fan of knots
the world seeps through, like a catch in the river's throat,

a speech almost speech, these cranes, in long
and longer loops of descent, settling finally among the reeds

sharp as bamboo. Their shadows seem to rise from the river
like hulls of boats. While the sails are borne from sky.

Unkind, Inclement Month

Cleaving is both ax stroke and embrace,
green in all directions—lightning rising
from the ground with the look of falling.

Open your heart to me, sap-thick, rung—

leaf, lichen, first seed—thrown to the ground.
Whole sentences of gnarled twig, still green
Four days of nor'easters, five of rain. The trees open.

Shifting Light/Columbia River Gorge

The Buddha was still small and stiff, one brass hand raised
over the bed sheets; the old mirror returning the far wall

with its usual disregard for exactitude. There was no gold
in the morning light. A lighter dark seeped through the blinds.

A single car rushed the empty street, a river over sand.
You were coming out of water, again. Rivulets of hair, dark grain.

I was picking blackberries, careful with my naked body
among so many stinging thorns. A mother led her calf to the river

but it stood crying on the sand and wouldn't go in
until you swam upriver, small as a stranger.

The berries weren't ripe, hard, heavy-seeded, hardly
a temptation. We were twenty. I was planning a pie, sweetening

what was sour. I remember that summer. A girl died in the same river,
tangled in the roots of the trees clear cut from Native lands.

Her body pulled down in the snow melt and backwash
of the nuclear power plant upriver in Washington. Mount St. Helens,

newly topless, smoked. It's a sin to let time sugar the past.
Behind the fridge the mat of hair and dry milk I never cleaned.

Let the mill at the bottom of the sea, endlessly churning salt,
preserve us as we were,

so we can arrive at this morning, a finger of dawn gold
traveling from the eastern window, across the pillow and into our eyes.

Lilies of the field

It is love or
some cousin. The same strange family—
genus, species, kingdom.

When you reach my heart, Lily,
I will awaken from the dream my golden-
fingered father read into me, stamen by stamen.

Water table at the soft place,
elbow's hinge, tangle of touch, root splayed
to petal, your palm's corolla.

Tales of the Sisters: Mermaids

I am fifteen. My body is swelling like the bloated belly of a dead fish. My sisters are not singing now. They are floating just there, beyond me. Mute.

They have cut their hair, given their tongues, and bought me this voice. It has a fine, sharp double edge. Whatever I do with it must be permanent and indelible, like murder.

"Do it," they say in gestures, "Or we'll be nothing but foam."

But, my darlings, this is all I can do.

the mystic crucifixion by Tintoretto

has become a Nativity. A curator's x-ray reveals the bishop below
the shepherd, hands folded over his heart. The woman
with her arms flung wide has not lost her son, but received
him—suffering at both ends of the frame, worn
canvas sewn together. A chicken scratches
in the dirt. Over the hill the Magi arrive, impossibly clean
like a cavalry of peace. They have left their arms
at the palace, hands clasped around enthusiasm already
brimming the small vessel that must contain it. His
swaddling is whiter than the lamb
that sniffs at its fold. To work this miracle the legs of Christ
are severed, painted over. An angel is chopped in half. Clouds
become rocks. Everything heavier as the glory settles
like sediment in a glass. A camel spits.
Crickets stitch in the straw. It is always the first day.

Corpse Pose

At *Shavasana*, my father crouched down
at my shoulder and stroked my face
with a touch so stripped of the toying
I knew in life, of anything but tenderness
and selfless grief that I...what shall I say?
        I don't know this I who could
accept that touch, who could trust it.

There was water somehow, a stream.
We were in a wood, in summer.
Water, tree shadow, evening light,
the last bit of the day, dusk creeping up
from the water sound, which never stopped.

I pressed the vision to stay. I wanted
to see that face, rinsed of all
that ailed him, tortured him really.
        He was there for me, *this* me,
knew my troubles. He had come for me.

As though I were the dead one.

Inauguration

inaugurare: to foretell the future from the flight of birds

The footnotes are in without a paragraph
for this morning's sparrow. He means

the nest is still his, and the branch, and the morning's
traffic surf, with a far-off siren's windy mourning.

He sings like our noise is weather, like we haven't been
here long, and won't be. It's a warm day. He husbands

his branch. Soon it will leaf—bright squirrel ear
to dark hand. The neighbor's ginger cat, too fat and fearful

to hunt, will roll in the dust of summer. The speckled
song this bird goes on about will fledge.

Tilth of snow

Polar bears in an almost empty zoo.
My child, so recently a four-footed animal, now two,
in her first real coat, bright red corduroy

like the bear in the book.

In an icy underground room
two busloads of fur—impossibly large—swim
and beat paws big as drumheads

against thick glass, which shivers.

In another room, another glass,
another bear—on dry land, collected, glossy—
looking maybe at us, maybe, its reflection,

maybe, at the snow. Reading.

I turn to a plaque
while my child, in her cardinal's coat,
stares with the patience of a Buddha

at the bear. Turn again

and it's already done,
young mother easily distracted, inattentive,
Bear running, a blur. Prey cut from the herd.

Only the glass, shivering,

prevents the clean, white fact.
The child devours the hungry bear in the glass
as it turns—

Good bear. Beautiful bear.

Heaven

Finally I am ready for heaven. Go ahead,
let it in now. I stare at winter branches
and try to imagine summer—all that green,
early urgency to late summer flapping
a crowd, a host.

                  I never had the time
before, never saw the point. I was getting
ready for the next thing, saving up.
Death might, I know, come quickly,
but that's not the main thing.

Something is leaking in, and I
can clear the way, make it easier
for it to enter. Yes. I'm saying yes.
Not to death, which isn't really my
business, but to heaven.

It may be that I'll be a scattering
of matter. It may be that I don the robe,
whatever that is. This morning
I wrap the gray wool light around me
and say to everyday morning sounds,
you can tell me everything now. All of it.

The Dead Wait on the Living to Go on Living

The chairs wide-mouthed and silent in each other's presence;
the cat crosses the floor, walking to the single shaft of sun.
I have come up the dark stairs, small, like the iceman,
milkman, the grocer's son, day's maid, shoulders brushing
plaster. The home breaks down so frequently, the future
depends more than ever on the teaching body. It's late;
afternoon sun behind clouds the color of pearl and pussy willows,
cars hurtling home. Soon you will come home, hungry;
you will open the fridge and frown, find the milk, pour
a mug and sweeten it. The clay mask you made me
—marble eyes, a purple skin—has fallen under a load of books.
A bell, like a buoy, marks this window's harbor. Among the mild
gray attics, all sheep, only the church is steep and belled
—mischievous goat. This isn't thinking, ticking the world off
lamb by lamb. Cold, counting fingers close my eyes,
two dead coins. But here you are announcing yourself, just
as I'd imagined: "I'm home!" smelling like wood smoke and leaves.
There is something the living say, something under my tongue,
but you're already past me, shedding your coat, radiating warmth.

It's simpler

to say let the water rise up
and cup itself in the sand,
let time run out, let moths
shake the dust from their wings
against the hot bulb.

                          Stop
repeating the old admonitions,
the notes to self. The mind
is full of tar. It's almost solid
or suggests a solid, as mercury
suggests steel, and these clouds
stones.

                    Where are the accusers?
They have gone home, touched
their hands to the lintel, ducked
their heads. They don't know
what to pray. There is no salt,
no curse, no bone. Mercy
has taken it all away.

Lifting Heaven from Its Shelf

Blue of sky, blue of snow, blue rattle of spring pane in autumn's window;
a lock trips, bone over blue bone, no harm done—that's first—nothing broken.

Blue of sky, blue of snow, blue of shadow still wet with the dark that evening
left there, even after the first birds, blue children of birds, call up the sun

pale blue egg—first egg, egg against which all other eggs are drawn,
still warm, resting in the palm, a trembling, a tapping claw, blind man's cane.

O blue in the skull where I laid my lord and lost him, blue of the virgin's cloak,
blue in the bucket. I will drown for lack of this blue, hard-pressed by other

colors. The raccoon washes his paws in a blue burnt black, and starlight
is rinsed in it also. If I could bathe in that pool, there would be no more poems

for me, but only blue, pouring its restless cure into my waiting ear.

Author photograph by Frank J. Garcia.

Kim Garcia is the author of *The Brighter House*, winner of the 2015 White Pine Press Poetry Prize; *DRONE*, winner of the 2015 Backwaters Prize; and *Madonna Magdalene*, released by Turning Point Books in 2006. Her chapbook *Tales of the Sisters* won the 2015 Sow's Ear Poetry Review Chapbook Contest. Her poems have appeared in such journals as *Crab Orchard Review, Crazyhorse, Mississippi Review, Nimrod*, and *Subtropics,* and her work has been featured on *The Writer's Almanac.* Recipient of the 2014 Lynda Hull Memorial Prize, an AWP Intro Writing Award, a Hambidge Fellowship and an Oregon Individual Artist Grant, Garcia teaches creative writing at Boston College.

THE WHITE PINE PRESS POETRY PRIZE